A Quick Guide to Video Coaching

The best practice to improve the art and craft of teaching through guided reflection

Jim Thompson

Casey Kosiorek

FOREWORD

I had been a classroom teacher for 22 years when I first heard about Video Coaching. Imagining video-recording myself teaching and sharing it with another professional intrigued me and frightened me at the same time. Since I'd never actually seen myself teach before, I was interested; yet I was also a bit apprehensive about that very same thing.

No longer a newbie, I had to admit that my instructional strategies had gotten stale. I had become comfortable in my style, and since I'd always received the satisfactory/effective rating on any formal observations, I kind of figured, "If it ain't broke..."

My curiosity, thankfully, got the better of me, and I decided to engage in this new type of individualized professional development to help get me out of the rut that I don't think I even knew I was stuck in.

I emailed my superintendent at that time, Dr. Casey Kosiorek; a pioneer in video coaching, and a huge proponent of purposeful teaching and self-reflection. He quickly put me in touch with video coach, Mr. Jim Thompson; a 30 year veteran in education and the Executive Director of Video Coaching for the Genesee Valley Educational Partnership. With the help of these two gentlemen and their vision, I was inspired and guided while learning more about my practice than I ever thought possible.

Think for a second...you look in the mirror every day. On some days, you see your reflection and are happy with the face smiling back at you. You share your confident feeling with someone you care about, and they reflect that positivity back to you! On other days, you see your reflection and immediately try to fix what you don't like. Then, you get a second opinion (although I wouldn't recommend a teenage daughter). A person you trust and have built a relationship with helps you discover why `Boot A' looks better than `Boot B.' Together you discuss the reasons, and you make the final decision that best reflects your goal of looking your finest.

Now imagine reflecting on your teaching using Video Coaching. You see yourself on video. There will be parts of the video that build your confidence and make you feel proud of your abilities and competence. You share that reaction with an experienced coach, who reflects that positivity back to you! A video coach who makes you feel valued, respected, appreciated, and validated.

And then there will be parts of the video that might surprise you. You may have questions, want guidance or encouragement; or maybe you just want to ask someone else for his/her opinion. Someone you trust and have built a relationship with that will help you discover why `Strategy A' works better than `Strategy B.' Together you discuss the reasons or the theory, and you alone make the decision that best reflects your goal of improving your instructional practice and student learning.

That's why A Quick Guide to Video Coaching is such a treasure to all teachers wishing to enhance and improve their instruction. The book thoroughly explains how to use video technology and trained coaches to bring teachers to their best selves. As the book states, "...inspire teachers to do more than they think they can."

A Quick Guide to Video Coaching is unique in that it offers practical, effective, easy-to-follow and ready-to-use steps that will guide school districts through the process of developing a successful video coaching program to improve teaching and student learning. The book shares several teachers' actual experiences with video coaching and clearly reveals the transformations that positively affected their individual growth. Mr. Thompson and Dr. Kosiorek's "Secret Sauce" recipe thoroughly clarify the six ingredients necessary for an effective video coaching program. The authors, who have spearheaded this approach in many school districts since 2012, also share their Big Ideas to help your district begin this worthwhile and rewarding journey, while continuously emphasizing confidentiality and teacher self-reflection.

I am a firm believer in this process and have personally experienced and witnessed the effectiveness of video coaching. In fact, I began training with Mr. Thompson in 2015 to become a Video Coach. We are now in our 5th year of video coaching at Byron-Bergen and have 80% of our faculty, K-12 involved in this purposeful, relevant and ongoing individualized professional development.

By following the advice and steps outlined in A Quick Guide to Video Coaching and stressing the aforementioned "Secret Sauce" ingredients, your teachers will discover, along with a trained coach, the very best methods needed to ensure that every day is valuable for every student.

Debbie Slocum, Video Coach
Byron-Bergen Central School District

CONTENTS

ACKNOWLEDGMENTS

Collaboration comes in many forms, and experience is never gained in isolation.

This book was made possible by the valuable interactions we both have enjoyed over decades of working with school administrators, teachers, support staff, students, and parents -- all of whom have added to our repertoire as professionals. We have learned from national consultants and colleagues in New York State. Our journey has led us to friendships that have made us better educators and better people. We thank you all.

Throughout this odyssey, our families continue to shine above us, as steadily and humbly as the North Star. For their unwavering support, we are forever grateful.

Jim and Casey

INTRODUCTION

The need to train high school graduates specifically to become teachers was recognized in the early 1800s. Over the next century, "normal schools" turned into teachers' colleges which became state universities, and these entities changed from teacher training schools to liberal arts colleges and then into research universities. The focus reasonably shifted from the practical to the theoretical as a result of this evolution. Many colleges and universities have attempted to recalibrate their approach to preparing prospective teachers for the profession, but it is evident that teacher preparation must continue to evolve with more emphasis on teaching experiences that provide opportunities for feedback and reflection on a continuous basis.

It's not just our postgraduate teaching preparatory programs that struggle with this mission; the field of K-12 education owns a big part of this dilemma as well. Once teacher candidates enter the system, we continue to miss the target by not providing opportunities for them to improve their instruction. The structure and methods for such approaches are absent from the field. Often quality professional development is sparse and may seem more like a current fad rather than a change in practice for overall teaching improvement.

Early on in our approach, we were convinced the answer could be found in the realm of coaching. One of us had some experience with peer coaching where colleagues meticulously "scripted" each other's lessons and provided feedback within carefully agreed-upon parameters. The other had experience as a student-athlete through college, varsity coach, and physical education teacher who recalled an expression repeated by a football coach: "The eye in the sky doesn't lie." The football coach was referring to video-recording.

That's when we experimented with the notion of recording a teacher's instruction. A curious and willing classroom teacher had video-recorded a number of his lessons and allowed us to view them. Then we sat down together to discuss exactly what we were seeing. The teacher was energized by the undeniable evidence of his own actions, both those that were effective and those that were not. We discovered that the teacher, who was seeing himself teach for the first time, was very capable of identifying those teacher actions that needed to be altered to produce more desirable results, but the lightbulb went off when we realized that the experience could be enriched with the guidance of an instructional expert.

We started small with "slow is fast" as our mantra. In the first year, we worked with about a half dozen volunteer teachers. Fourteen teachers benefitted from video coaching the next year. Within four years, the number of schools participating had increased dramatically. We know the video coaching approach is working as part of systemic change because we are now training cadres of coaches instead of only working with individual classroom teachers. Part of our journey has been understanding how important quality control at every juncture is in maintaining credibility and building trust.

In this book, we are offering a pragmatic approach to the implementation of a video coaching model in your school. We have successfully worked through our model on a small scale in a small school, then on a larger scale in a small school, then in nine different school districts, and now on a larger scale in a large school district.

The most direct route to improved instruction is to refocus and support teachers on their teaching by having them reflect on their own practice in a safe environment with a trained coach in response to incontrovertible video evidence of the instruction they deliver in their own classrooms. We're excited about helping you to chart your own course.

WHAT IS VIDEO COACHING?

Video coaching is a form of teacher professional development that we believe is what the field has been clamoring for. How do we support and grow more fruitful conversations between teachers about instruction with all the other distractions in the profession? How do schools support teachers implementing new instructional strategies in their classrooms? How do schools honor the art and craft of teaching? How does the field of education at all levels improve pedagogy that ultimately influences student outcomes? We believe video coaching is the answer.

Video coaching is the use of video-recording technology to complement the work a teacher is engaging in with an instructional coach. Let's delve into what an instructional coach is for those who are not as familiar with the term.

In education, terms like cognitive coaching, executive coaching, content coaching, literacy coaching, and peer coaching often are used interchangeably without the user's complete understanding (Knight, 2007). Knight (2007) described instructional coaching as the relationship an instructional specialist has with a teacher in which evidence-based best teaching strategies are incorporated into a participating teacher's approach to instruction. A coaching relationship relies on a cycle of feedback exchange between the coach and the teacher. The coach's responsibility is to support teachers by helping them draw conclusions about their teaching practice through reflection (Knight, 2007). Reflection is only possible after an instructional coach and teacher have developed a positive exchange of trust, good communication, and specific feedback (Knight, 2007). The coach acts as a guide, providing instructional tips, ideas, and encouragement.

King et al. (2014), working for The Annenberg Institute for School Reform at Brown University (hereafter Annenberg Institute), viewed instructional coaching as a teacher development approach in which classroom instructors were trained to provide feedback and modeling to other teachers. The Annenberg Institute endorsed the instructional coaching model because the approach was strongly aligned with its core framework regarding what makes professional development valuable. The framework held that the training applies to many grade levels of instruction in a school, has the potential to develop human talent, and must be sustainable (King et al., 2014).

Knight (2007) summed up instructional coaching when he described an instructional coach as a professional developer who uses research-proven instructional strategies to support teachers in the art and craft of teaching. He went on to describe a coaching cycle as a series of events that includes the coach meeting with the teacher to explain the objectives of coaching and the teacher sharing what will be taught and what, hopefully, the students will accomplish during the lesson. This conversation includes lesson objectives, standards, assessments, and learning activities (Knight, 2007). The coach and the teacher discuss what they believe will be the best instructional strategies to accomplish the desired student learning outcomes. The coach welcomes and encourages questions from the teacher and provides an opportunity to share the teacher's needs or desired areas of focus (Knight, 2007). After the lesson is completed, the coach and the teacher discuss what occurred during instruction, celebrating the sections of the teacher's instruction that went well and discussing areas of the teacher's instruction that can improve. The coach's goal is to tease out areas of improvement after the teacher has reflected on the lesson (Knight, 2007). The next step is for the coach to recommend and model instructional strategies for the teacher to implement (Knight, 2007). The feedback cycle is intended to be ongoing.

Now let's layer on the use of video-recording technology to complement the instructional coaching process. In our model, teachers utilize video to record their instruction. We utilize the Swivl robot (www.swivl.com) partnered with an iPad or smartphone. The teachers start by recording a portion of a lesson, then review and reflect on what they have observed by themselves and complete a written reflection. Once the written reflection is completed it is shared with the video coach. This provides important information to the coach as the teacher and coach enter into their first coaching conference. The teacher and video coach then meet in person to discuss the reflection. This is the baseline of the process. The meeting takes place prior to discussing what they would like to focus on in future recording and coaching sessions. In the video coaching model, the coach is not present during the recording of teaching as the goal of the recording is to capture the teacher's instruction in the most organic state. This is one difference from the instructional coaching model. When the lesson recording is completed it is then uploaded to the Swivl video software so that the teacher and coach can view the video separately, reflect on it and comment on what they observed. The teacher and coach then meet to discuss the lesson and agree on areas for growth and strategies for improvement.

Seems simple right? It is, but it takes applying the strategic steps that we have learned from our implementation to be successful. We believe that video coaching is the most meaningful approach to improve instruction for teachers in public, charter, private, and university education. The goal of video coaching is to re-culture your learning institution one instructor at a time.

Don't believe us, that's okay; hear what teachers who have participated in video coaching are experiencing in the process. During our work, we have collected copious amounts of information. We have conducted surveys and interviewed teachers who have participated in the video coaching approach that we have implemented, and here is what they are sharing about their experience:

"I thought it was an awesome experience in reflecting and improving instruction. I found this to be more motivating than any other professional development that I've ever participated in before."

~ *Susan*

"Even without the feedback of the coach, I was motivated to make changes based on the videos that I watched myself. I felt like I really wanted to do something to improve my instruction after observing myself teach. It was extremely motivational and meaningful."
~ *Michael*

"Video coaching is non-threatening, motivating, and do-able. It's very flexible. It's inspiring -- you see what you are doing well and have some practical applications for getting better in weaker areas."
~ *John*

"It helped me see the physical spaces of my classroom and see instructional practices that were and were not working. It was a quality program that allowed me to truly reflect on my teaching and make improvements for not only me but for my students as well."
~ *Mary*

"Reflecting and making instructional decisions with someone who is removed from the classroom environment and is an instructional expert was beneficial. Getting students involved allowed me to view their engagement and understanding of content."
~ *Brian*

"I think this is a great tool for our teaching staff. It has the ability to highlight instruction in a non-threatening, growth-oriented way. The ability to see your teaching in a new way -- clearly removes assumptions about how instruction is presented. New strategies from an experienced instructor are presented which adds to the toolbox. Goals are set after the first video versus the past when goals were set based on what teacher thought was an area in need of growth -- these goals are set with concrete evidence. It was a liberating experience knowing one could try new approaches without formal evaluation being involved."

~ *Sarah*

"Given time to reflect with a professional on ways to improve teaching was more meaningful than reading a rubric score. Reviewing your own teaching by playing back the recording to see the events within the lesson, ability to reflect on goals, specific students, and the way I interacted with students was so powerful."

~ *Julie*

"The advantages are that you can see yourself teach. You don't know what you look like when you teach. At first, I didn't like watching myself, but once I got over that, it was very powerful. It gives you a huge advantage into your growth as an educator."

~ *Aaron*

"The concept that seeing yourself on video was very helpful to the reflection process. The power is that you can't help but agree with some of it and disagree with some of it because it is right in front of your face.

It provides real evidence, not subjective thoughts."

~ *Scott*

"Sometimes during a lesson, I get so into my teaching that it is difficult to remember certain aspects. By capturing it on video, it alleviates this and makes reflection better."

~ *William*

"It often affirmed and confirmed things that I do well and also helped me identify areas for improvement. I learned different techniques in college, and I didn't always know if I was utilizing them the way they were intended to be used. After working with the coach, he helped me see that, indeed, I was using them appropriately."

~ *Joe*

"I appreciated that it wasn't a one-and-done professional development. This was the first time that it applied to what I do and I can keep participating until I stop teaching, and I plan to."

~ *Sean*

"The coach had formed a partnership throughout the process. He helped me see things in myself that I was unable to see. He had a way of guiding me to find my own answers. I felt like we were learning together."

~ *Matt*

"I met with the coach, and he was great. He first helped me celebrate the things I did well. He then helped me identify areas for improvement. More importantly, he shared and modeled the strategies we discussed. This element of the program is very important, and I think it would look very different if it were just reflection without an instructional specialist guiding the process."

~ *Donna*

"I've learned more from these discussions, and I've retained it because immediately the next day after I spoke to the coach and went back and I tried something that he told me, and I've used it ever since."

~ *Philip*

"One of the things that I really like about the program is it doesn't feel like additional work that is above and beyond."

~ *Lynn*

"I love the fact that I can automatically use a strategy or new approach and apply it to my teaching after a coaching session. Then I record myself again and share it with the coach, and we do it again and again until I master it. It is a constant cycle of feedback."

~ *Melanie*

"I have kept a journal after I have taught a lesson and then sat back and thought about how I could improve on it, but the use of video puts you in a whole different league as far as reflection."
~ *Ethan*

"I was seeing what the students saw. It really challenged my thinking, the way I look at things. I thought a lot about what I saw. I shared what I reflected on with my coach. The ability to reflect was very, very powerful. I loved that this was a confidential process."
~ *Adam*

Teachers have individual perceptions of how they believe they teach or what they look like when teaching. The video-recording provides participants the opportunity to see what their students experience. It provides them the opportunity to pause, rewind, and comment during the process of reflection. Very few of the teachers we have worked with have had the chance to capture their instruction in this way.

The use of video-recording technology also contributes to teachers' interaction with their instruction and reflection on their practice as a result of viewing the recorded session because teachers and coaches review the recording multiple times, pausing it, marking it, and unpacking what took place. This leads to a more comprehensive analysis of what occurred during the lesson. It is rare for someone to remember every single detail and experience without video.

Teachers recognize video coaching's positive impact on their instruction. They find it to be an effective program, unlike any other approach they have experienced in the past. There have been few opportunities in education that provide them the opportunity to view themselves teach and observe what their students experience during their instruction. There have not been methods that provide a mechanism to memorialize interactions during a lesson between the teacher and their students and students with their classmates. Teachers found value in capturing instruction on video, the reflective process, and recognized that — although self-reflection is necessary and can improve their skills — the video coach enhances their experience. Teachers identify areas for growth through the process and confirm the opportunity to celebrate individual strategies that work well. Teachers embrace the value of video coaching being embedded and ongoing in their work with students.

Teachers share that the coach is an integral factor in the quality of the coaching program. Relationship building between the coach and teachers is critical. The coach needs excellent communication skills to truly make a difference. Coaches need to have the ability to help a teacher to notice areas for growth in a thoughtful manner. The coach questions and teases out details in the reflection process, and this takes a commitment to skill development.

The coach should be knowledgeable, non-threatening, and welcoming. Coaches need to be everything we look for in a good friend, a partner, or a spouse. This includes being an active listener, possessing a high level of emotional intelligence, being respectful, honest, and able to cultivate a relationship of trust.

The secret sauce of video coaching

We believe that there are six ingredients in the secret sauce of a successful video coaching program that, along with the coach, are integral to the implementation and sustainability of quality video coaching. The ingredients included in the approach being: Non-evaluative, confidential, optional, embedded, ongoing, and reflective.

Non-evaluative

Although video coaching provides a systematic approach for a teacher to work with a coach to evaluate his or her practice, it should be non-evaluative in the sense that the teacher is not rated for the purpose of making an employment decision. Once teachers recognize that the coaching process is a safe environment, they are more likely, to be honest with themselves and the coach. Teachers and coaches should know what they share will have no impact on their employment or their future with the organization.

Confidential

Confidentiality is closely aligned with the program being non-evaluative. Whatever is discussed in the coaching cycle between the teacher and coach needs to remain between the two as this element supports the risk-taking and vulnerability necessary to grow through the video coaching model. We often refer to this aspect of the program as the coach acting like the participant's priest, rabbi, or counselor. Your program most likely will come to a screaming halt if the coach shares the content of the coaching sessions with other teachers or the principal. Trust is the glue that fortifies the climate necessary for teachers to embrace this concept and begin to appreciate that this is not a program attempting to catch someone doing something wrong, but rather a supportive approach that requires openness and honesty.

Optional participation

Optional participation means that teachers have the choice of whether or not they will participate in the program. The fact that the program is not mandated or forced on teachers is an important element to its success, especially in the early implementation stage.

Embedded

We all need to be learning at all times. When a skill is a part of our daily learning and is meaningful to the work we do, it becomes important to us. The skills and feedback that are gained from video coaching must be applied immediately to teachers' instruction with students. This application provides a teacher with the opportunity to practice the newly learned skills in an authentic environment.

Ongoing

Ongoing refers to the concept that teachers apply feedback to their practice on a continuous basis. Video coaching cycles are encouraged to continue until the day a teacher leaves the profession. The goal is to be in a continuous state of improvement.

Reflective

Having the opportunity and skills to look back at an action and think about it is an important part of improving. The use of video provides a recording similar to the methods used in athletics. Whether it is improving your golf swing, identifying who missed his block in a football game or improving your teaching, reflection is a key part of the process.

WHY DO TEACHERS NEED VIDEO COACHING?

Why do teachers need video coaching? That is a great question. Whether in theory or action, most would agree that the teacher makes the difference with student success. Arguably, we can debate other factors that may influence the learning process, but at the end of the day, the quality of the teacher has the greatest impact on students. We believe this is true from relationship building with students and their families to the instructional strategies and assessment methods used in the learning process. We want teachers to be great every single day by knowing the most effective way to reach all of their students. Teachers put their blood, sweat, and tears into their work, and parents put their trust in our teachers to teach their children.

Most professions have a rigorous approach to learning their trades, whether it is developing the skills to become a mechanic or a dentist. We all want the best. We wouldn't go to a second-rate physician if we had a serious health condition or a subpar attorney if our conviction depended on it. Somehow teachers slip through the cracks. Doctors go through a year of residency after four years of medical school. Other professionals serve in positions with increasing levels of responsibilities with direct supervision and feedback every step of the way. We owe teachers more than what they're getting. When do teachers receive this support?

Not all, but many of the experiences teachers have once they have entered the field with professional development fall in one of the following categories:

- Much of the professional development time is spent in a lecture format — "sit 'n git" — with a great deal of theory and little or no attention to what good instruction looks like and how to make it happen consistently.
- Many professional developers do not have the expertise with classroom instruction or have not been in the classroom for many years.
- Teachers rarely have the chance to work in a guided systematic approach on why a lesson did or did not "go well."
- Principals meet with teachers to review lesson plans, but the conferencing about teaching often comes after observing several lessons, so feedback is often generic ("You are doing a good job with transitions between activities so little time is wasted" or "Be sure to wait a few seconds after asking a question of the class to give everyone time to formulate an answer.") Helpful information, to be sure, but seldom are comments connected to a specific action which can be replicated or applied.
- Teachers never see what they are doing actually looks like — good or bad.
- There simply are not enough opportunities to talk about good instruction — to see it modeled, to practice it, and get specific feedback.

Video-recording has a positive impact on teaching

Romano and Schwartz (2005) researched video-recording teaching, online discussions, and portfolio development to identify which practice was perceived to be most beneficial for teachers. Participants said that video-recording helped them identify unintentional tendencies that they would not have observed otherwise. Video-recording provided feedback to support their improvement (Romano & Schwartz, 2005).

Participants in video-recording felt that this approach identified concrete evidence and behaviors that required modification to improve their teaching. Tripp and Rich (2012) reviewed 63 studies that examined the use of video in teachers' self-reflection. When instructors were asked whether they found video-recording valuable to their profession, the majority indicated that it was beneficial. The results included teachers' satisfaction with the process in each study and provided evidence that video-recording led to teachers' increased desire to change practice (Tripp & Rich, 2012).

Video-recording enhances self-analysis and reflection

There are many methods that can be used by teachers to reflect on their practice. Developing a teacher portfolio and journaling are some of the most popular approaches. Creating a portfolio provides the instructor a system to record practices over time. The shortfall of the teaching portfolio concept is that it does not take place in real time and often is focused on celebrating good teaching and not necessarily on identifying areas for growth (Felder & Brent, 1996). Video coaching captures teaching in the moment and encourages celebrating good teaching while also identifying areas for growth.

Self-reflection through narrative journaling is an approach based on the work of John Dewey. It involves writing down thoughts about a recent experience and sharing the entry with a journal reader who provides feedback (Hubbs & Brand, 2005). The act of reflective journaling as a tool for learning provides teachers with an opportunity to revisit their actions and identify common themes in their teaching, and provides them a mechanism to grapple with different ideas and approaches that can be applied in the future based on their memory of what is being reflected on (Hubbs & Brand, 2005).

Although a valid method for professional growth, reflective journaling does not provide the opportunity for teachers to see what their students see. The video provides a lens that allows the teacher to view classroom instruction from different perspectives. When teachers have the opportunity to observe what their students experienced, they developed a more reflective approach to their teaching.

Participating in video analysis and reflection increases teachers' desire to change their teaching. Tripp and Rich (2012) studied the effects of teachers viewing their teaching on video and whether it led to reflection on a more regular basis. The study measured a teacher's profile at the beginning and end of the project to assess the teacher's ability to reflect using a pre and post questionnaire. Twelve of the 13 teachers agreed that they experienced an improved ability to reflect on their practice and that video-recording was helpful (Tripp & Rich, 2012).

The important skill of noticing during video reflection

A teacher must establish a strong capacity to identify what best teaching practices are before video-recording can be used as an effective approach to improve a teacher's pedagogy (Baecher & Kung, 2011). This skill is necessary when teachers observe a video-recording of their instruction for the sake of improvement. For example, imagine if an instructor had not received the appropriate training and practice in classroom management strategies. If this instructor believed that it was unnecessary for a classroom to have some order or management systems to support student learning, then the instructor may struggle to understand or recognize what good classroom management practice is. This affirms the need for a video coach in the reflection process.

Baecher and Kung (2011) focused on student teachers' inability to identify areas of improvement when observing their recorded instruction. The findings supported the concept that teachers need to develop an increased awareness of their actions and improve their ability to describe learning if their goal was to improve their teaching through video-recording. Baecher and Kung (2011) defined this skill as the teacher's ability to notice. The ability to notice when using video-recording to improve teaching is instrumental in the development of both novice and veteran teachers and why the video coach plays such an important role in this model.

Star and Strickland (2008) focused on a teacher's ability to notice and to note what is taking place in the classroom during the teacher's instruction. This perspective drilled deeper into the area of instructional strategies. For example, instructional strategies consist of techniques used to check for student engagement and understanding of a learning objective or what a teacher should do when students are learning at different rates within a lesson.

King (2008) studied video-recording teaching practices and found that it also had a positive influence on the teacher's ability to notice. Reflection can occur without the use of video, but video and the use of video coaching enhances the reflection experience because it provides concrete evidence and an instructional expert to guide the process. Many teachers do not know what they look like when they are teaching (Knight, 2014), and this experience augments the reflective process.

Along with the use of video to enhance reflection is the role of the instructional coach who guides the reflection process throughout the coaching cycle (Knight, 2007). Shewell (2013) explored the attitudes of instructional coaches when using the Datacapture recording software to collect video-based evidence in a teacher's lesson. The study found that although both coaches and teachers perceived video-recording as effective, coaches required training to provide feedback in a safe and non-evaluative manner to prevent having a negative impact on the school culture (Shewell, 2013).

The evidence presented in this literature supported the idea that a teacher's ability to notice along with their level of withitness could impact how successful they are when using video-recording as a tool for improvement. These skills, when developed at least at a basic level, will support efforts to use video to improve teacher practice in K-12 education.

WHAT MAKES A GOOD VIDEO COACH?

Putting donuts in the faculty room on Fridays does not build school culture. Competence creates a positive school culture. Glowing tweets on social media highlighting the fabulous activities happening in a school do not automatically translate into how people feel every day.

We have spent a great deal of time looking at the video coaches we have been training over the past couple of years, watching for similarities in personality, background, experience, education, and temperament. While we don't believe, necessarily, that good video coaches are born, there are some innate characteristics that facilitate the work and provide a solid basis for advanced training. Caring, connected, and competent are good places to start.

When it comes to being an effective video coach, a genuine concern, and respect for teachers and what they do every day is paramount. Educators can be some of the most sensitive people we know and take it personally when we talk about their professional practice. Teachers who are working with a coach need to believe that they are operating in an environment that has their best interests at the core of every interaction.

Teaching often is an isolated act. We've heard teachers say, "Just give me my students and let me close my door and teach." In our own backgrounds, we've experienced programs that attempt to open that closed door and decrease the isolation — mentoring, peer observation and coaching, co-teaching, to name a few.

Three decades ago, a move to bring teachers together to talk about instruction took shape under the titles "peer observation" and "peer coaching," the first suggesting back-and-forth, anecdotal feedback between two colleagues watching each other teach and the second implying that one teacher is empowered to offer suggestions to another. Like in co-teaching models, the relationship between professional peers can be complicated. At a minimum, extensive training, careful pairings, and crystal clear guidelines must be established and evaluated, but the time and resources rarely are provided to make these programs work to their potential. Peer support can often look like a mutual admiration society so that no one's feelings are bruised; at its worst, it can become two suspicious teachers, each wondering "who died and left the other in charge."

Soliciting advice is risky business. Olympic athletes may watch others who compete in the same sport to get some ideas about form or technique, but when they genuinely want to perform better, they ask the coach, not a peer.

To extend the analogy, an Olympic coach knows that their players are at the top of their sport, having spent years learning, practicing, and refining their skills. But the best athletes seek their coaches' input and makes changes to their performance in order to get a better result. Competition at this level is emotional and stressful, so the athlete depends on the coach to connect personally, provide inspiration to excel, and emphasize continuous growth. A great coach inspires players to do more than they think they can. This is true in sports, in entertainment (think: acting or voice coach), in business — and in teaching.

Knowing when to push is as important as knowing how to push. Choosing the correct time to implement coaching feedback and the prioritization of what feedback to give are challenging skills that take someone with high emotional intelligence and outstanding communication skills. We all can point to examples of people who "weren't ready" to hear a suggestion. Once that happens, the circle of trust is broken and must be mended before any further coaching can occur. Certainly, an instructional coach needs to know which skills and strategies will move a teacher forward, but perception and intuition play a key role in determining when to introduce new ideas into a coaching relationship. With video coaching, the added piece of the teacher seeing a recorded "performance" in the classroom, possibly for the first time, may require the coach to step back and allow the teacher to get over the initial reaction. (As one of our teachers once said: "Who is that woman on the video and why does she look so terrible in my clothes?")

So, who are these people who make ideal video coaches? They are lifelong learners. You know these people. They work on themselves endlessly. "Good enough" is a phrase that does not exist in their repertoire. They are serial risk-takers, habitual readers, and eternal optimists.

They have a heightened sense of self-awareness. They know who they are. They pay attention to their own emotions and have fewer blind spots than most. They are reflective and can articulate what self-reflection has sparked in their own continuous growth.

They have a broad vision but can focus on important details. They see the forest and the trees. They don't allow the overload of fragmented pieces to skew their view; instead, they can integrate data into a context or framework and make a "whole" out of the parts.

They are a quick study. This is a slightly different quality than simply being "smart." A quick study learns new things rapidly and easily grasps all the details and nuances of a discussion or situation.

They believe coaching is a two-way exchange of ideas and learnings. They love the conversation. They are fifty percent of an improvement team, not the proverbial "sage on the stage." Coach and teacher are working together in a spirit of improvement.

They walk the walk and talk the talk. They need to come with a reputation for being knowledgeable and competent. They are able to offer concrete, pedagogically sound suggestions. They can translate theory into practice. Very simply, they know what they're talking about.

They have a sincere and selfless desire to help. Most educators thrive on helping others in a non-specific sense. The best video coaches choose this work because it helps teachers become better at their craft, one at a time. The rewards for the coach are much more intrinsic than for the teacher with whom the coach is collaborating.

"The coach makes a difference." We have heard that declaration in every school in which we've implemented video coaching.

Those of us who are parents know well how unique each child really is. Even if they are raised in the same house by the same people until they reach adulthood, they turn out differently. They develop different interests, they respond to the world around them in different ways. We all enter school or college or the world of work with these differences built in. Great video coaches develop relationships with teachers with a thorough understanding of this concept. This individual relationship building makes coaching a more effective professional process and lends itself to a richer experience for both the coach and the teacher because human beings feel more comfortable taking risks and receiving feedback under these circumstances (Joyce & Showers, 1996).

Joyce and Showers (1982) found several skills that were necessary for coaching including an emphasis on the importance of relationship building. The coach has to be able to develop relationships while understanding that people often see things differently, and the coach must be able to provide encouragement and clarity, identifying that a natural part of the coaching process is identifying areas for improvement. This relationship building makes coaching a more effective professional process and lends itself to a richer experience for both the coach and the teacher because people feel more comfortable taking risks and receiving feedback (Joyce & Showers, 1996). Choosing the correct time to implement coaching feedback is a challenging skill to develop. It is important for coaches to spend time becoming experts on instructional strategies and content so that they can model and prompt the teacher to times when it is appropriate to implement the new practice (Joyce & Showers, 1996).

Feger, Woleck, and Hickman (2004) supported the importance of a coach developing good communication skills, that coaching should be done in a safe environment that promoted risk-taking, and the coach's ability to build trust with the teacher is important. Their research suggested that coaches should be able to identify resources to be shared in coaching sessions, including resources on both content and proven teaching practices. Feger et al. (2004) noted that developing quality coaching was difficult; therefore, the number of good coaches in education was limited.

Knight (2007) acknowledged that coaching must be based on a partnership between the coach and the teacher and identified what quality coaches do. In a coaching session, a good coach develops an environment that maintains a balance of power. In this relationship, one person does not appear to be the teacher while the other is perceived as the learner; instead, they should be observed as equals working together to solve a problem (Knight, 2007). A good coach develops an environment that is safe, allowing the teacher to feel confident and comfortable in a setting of open communication. A good coach refrains from telling; instead, both the coach and teacher contribute to the conversation by sharing their perspectives (Knight, 2007). A good coach supports a teacher by giving appropriate time to apply a new strategy, understanding that coaching sessions are a time at which the teacher can learn and that the coach can learn from the interaction with the teacher, as well. A good coach is an active listener, listening to what the teacher is saying rather than thinking of how to respond while the teacher is speaking (Knight, 2007). A coach must "seek to understand before being understood" (Covey, 1989, p. 235). A coach who is a good listener can be more successful in teasing out the teacher's reflections.

Borman and Feger (2006) asserted that good instructional coaches have many qualities. Although coaching attributes are broad, they concluded that there were several overarching categories that align with quality coaching, including the coach's ability to communicate, their pedagogical experience and knowledge, and their ability to work with people (Borman & Feger, 2006).

Knight (2007) pointed out the importance of commitment to the professional development of coaches and how it can affect the success of the implementation of an instructional coaching program. Without a commitment to the development of coaches, a school risks wasting the resources of funding and time and presents teachers with ineffective strategies. Schools implementing coaching must be committed to the development of the coaches and provide time for coaches to practice refining their coaching skills (Gallucci, Van Lare, Yoon, & Boatright, 2010). They also discussed the element of "learning on the job" (p. 942) that takes place, which is necessary and plays an important role in the coach's development. Knight (2007) suggested the importance of hiring coaches with the openness to develop coaching skills and the drive to implement a coaching system. Time for coaches to stay current on instruction should be a non-negotiable characteristic of a quality coaching program (Knight,

2007).

There is no one size fits all training for video coaches because everyone enters the position in a different place, and these are somewhat uncharted waters. As mentioned earlier, becoming a quality video coach and utilizing the resources in the field are probably your best starting point. Some of our take-aways we have experienced that we found beneficial to the development of our video coaches include the following.

Use video to improve as a coach

What's good for the goose is good for the gander. As you establish yourself as a coach, attempt to record yourself in a coaching session. Early in a video coaching initiative, you may find it difficult to find volunteers, so you might record yourself in a mock coaching conference. Just like the teachers, you will be working with, this allows you to see what you look like when working through a coaching session. Conduct your own self-reflection. Practice with a trusted colleague. Hopefully, you will build trust so you can record your coaching conferences. Make sure when you get to this point, the teacher you are coaching understands that this is for your professional growth. This will resonate greatly with the person you are coaching in that you are modeling all aspects that make video coaching so powerful.

Practice with online videos

As you build your skill set of observing instruction, you need to practice, practice, and practice. If you do not have access to video-recorded instruction in your school, do what everyone does -- go to the web. With minimal time, you will be able to find both partial and full segments of video-recorded instruction online, some good and some not so good, but nothing's perfect. Taking the time to observe these videos and reflect before you get into your first coaching session is very important. When implementing the coaching process, we recommend taking several months of dedicated time to develop as a coach. We did it and it pays dividends. We compare it to painting a house: the paint is nice, but the quality of the paint job is all in the scraping and preparation.

Ask for feedback

Coaching is not for those with a big ego. It is just as much about the coach's growth as it is the teacher's growth. Be open to feedback. Ask questions of the educator you are working with. As you develop a relationship, it will be more natural to share thoughts. In the desired state of video coaching, the coach and teacher are equals. During the planning phase of implementation, it is important to have the person with the right attributes and soft skills in the coaching position, as mentioned earlier. When seeking candidates, remember the qualities we discussed. A coach is always growing and can learn more about instruction. The appropriate mindset is a key element as you identify who will serve as your coach.

Focus on your own professional development

Be hungry and lap it up! The video coach must be a lifelong learner. Read, read, and read some more. It is just as important to develop yourself as a coach as it is to hold coaching conferences. This is very difficult to balance but is important. It sounds intimidating, but it shouldn't be. It is a matter of finding and vetting resources. You don't have to know it all, but you have to take the time to connect teachers with research-proven strategies that will help them improve in the area you have agreed to focus on. Failure is okay. Some strategies may work well, other may not be the right fit, or the teacher feels uncomfortable applying them. As much as this is a systematic approach, it is also an adventure.

Form a coaching network

Although there may not be many video coaches in your area, there are most likely more instructional coaches. Video coaching is an enhancement of the instructional coaching model, so look for others to bounce ideas off, to blog or Skype with. The old adage of taking care of yourself before you can take care of others is at play here. A good idea is a good idea and should be shared to improve the education of our students. The relationship will also provide a support structure as there is most likely only going to be one video coach in a school or district during early implementation.

Role-play

Role-play can often be hokie, but we have found that when

training coaches, this can be one of the most powerful exercises. We usually use a fishbowl technique where we have a coach conduct a conference with a teacher. We try to present different types of teacher personalities and mindsets to the coach for each of the scenarios. We then have the other coaches provide feedback on what they hear and see. Similar to the video coaching model, they provide strengths and areas for growth. This process is two-fold in the sense that the coach in the exercise hones their skills, but the others on the outside of the fishbowl do as well and usually don't realize they are practicing their approach to providing feedback.

Not forcing it

If a coaching session is not going well or you seem to be struggling with the approach, there is no need to force it. Video coaching should be a natural process. In the desired state, the coach helps teachers find their own answers. It is fine if there are some growing pains early in the process.

Hear what you hear

Be a good listener and don't impose your beliefs on what the teacher may be sharing during the process. This can be misinterpreted by the teacher. Take things at face value and don't get caught up in any nonsense if it presents itself. There is always subjectivity when you are working with people, but often remind yourself that your role as a coach is an objective guide to support and grow with the teacher.

Encourage

Always maintain a positive outlook and approach to coaching. Although working with adults can be challenging, remember to keep things in perspective. Teachers only get better if they want to get better, and the teachers participating in this approach are most likely those people. When providing feedback, we like to use what we call the sandwich approach. Offer or tease out a positive comment or reflection, then an area for growth, and finish with a celebration of good teaching.

A SNEAK PEEK INTO A VIDEO COACHING SESSION

The teacher/coach conference is the centerpiece of the video coaching process. We sometimes need to remind video coaches who are just starting on this journey to avoid getting too wrapped up in the technology at the expense of the time and attention that must be given to the actual conference with the teacher. We want to take full advantage of all that Jim has learned throughout his years as a video coach with this "sneak peek" into the video conference via five Big Ideas that have ruled his successful practice.

Big Idea #1 - Always start with a face-to-face conversation.

Most teachers really don't know what it looks like when they are engaged in the act of teaching. They know what they do, but — under normal circumstances — they never see themselves as their students and others in the classroom see them. So, from the start, we are talking about a highly personal conversation. Professionals take it very personally when someone talks about their practice; we often can't separate what we do from who we believe we are.

A skilled coach needs to be up-close-and-personal with educators who are going to be examining themselves under the close scrutiny of recorded lessons. With video, a teacher isn't able to rationalize, "I'm sure I didn't say it that way" or "I don't remember doing it that way." Self-discovery isn't always easy, and the coach must be able to read the teacher for signs of discomfort, embarrassment, or resistance. The absolute best way to accomplish this is to be sitting in the same room with the teacher, and this is what we recommend. (Skype, FaceTime, Zoom, etc., are options, but they are best utilized a little further down the road.)

Trust building begins here. Teachers need to be able to read the coach's demeanor, too, as you promise confidentiality and explain that you are their coach, a learning partner, and not their evaluator. The first face-to-face is the chance for you to make a great first impression, to establish common ground, and to honor the art of teaching.

Big Idea #2 - Don't take 'em by surprise…take a "selfie" instead.

When Jim first started working with teachers in video coaching, he found himself asking them to identify instructional goals for themselves. This usually resulted in perplexed looks, periods of silence, sometimes uncomfortable starts and stops. The most common response was, "I don't know. What do you think I should work on?" In effect, Jim was taking teachers by surprise.

When he changed his approach to asking teachers instead to "take a selfie," (Best Foot Forward Project, 2013), the results were much more positive. Borrowing from the research done at Harvard University in its Best Foot Forward program, Jim began his sessions by asking participating teachers to use a smartphone to self-record a segment of a lesson in preparation for their work together.

The self-reflection is 10-15 minutes (no longer) of a lesson that the teacher alone views, sets aside for a while, then reviews and answers these questions in a written reflection:

- What did you learn?
- What surprised you?
- What goal or goals might you have to work on with your coach in a subsequent video-recorded lesson?
- What else do you want to share from viewing your self-reflection?

Self-reflections are less intimidating than the more formal recording of an entire lesson. With the advent of smartphone video capabilities and the popularity of posting videos to Instagram and Facebook, many teachers are used to seeing short clips of themselves and others on computer screens.

Big Idea #3 - Foster two-way communication right away.

When Jim first started to receive self-reflections from some teachers, he was not sure what to expect.

The responses from these folks were beyond belief! They were asked to video just 10-15 minutes of a lesson, reflect on it, and then share responses to a few of the questions that he posed. First off, most teachers did more than one self-reflection; in fact, one teacher did 13 of them before choosing one to discuss in her reflection!

The reflections were universally thoughtful and deserving of a response. The self-reflection written piece presents an opportunity for the coach to communicate on a very personal level with the teacher.

Below are some sample reflections.

Dear Jim,

Thank you for being willing to support my video coaching.

I have been teaching…for about 16 years now. I initially received my teaching certification in Physical Education in 1985, but I soon found out it was difficult to get a job in PE at that time. I worked for a few years in various capacities after college….I also went back to school for my PE Master's Degree.

…I stayed home for 12 years to parent and teach my [children] while they were young. …I started to substitute teach and decided to go back to school to get my elementary education teaching degree. While doing that, I held a variety of long-term substitute positions…and then was hired as a full-time teacher. I first taught grades 2-4 in a multi-age setting and then moved to the K-2 multi-age class, which then morphed to grade 1-2 multi-age classroom. And that is how I arrived at the current level I teach! Here I still am, hoping to finish out a 20+ year teaching career in the next 5-8 years.

I volunteered to participate in video coaching because I like to always be the best I can be and offer my students an engaging learning experience, where we learn together from each other. I also thought it would be rewarding to get professional feedback about my teaching. I try to foster a supportive learning environment where students can feel comfortable learning, communicating with each other and working out social issues. But most importantly, I want my students to love coming to school and getting engaged in our learning.

I was glad my first experience with video-recording was a practice session. I video-recorded numerous parts of my day to get a feel for the process. I teach in various locations within the classroom, which made it tricky to find a good location to place the camera. Sometimes I sit on the floor or stand and teach at the SmartBoard in the front of the room. I meet with small groups at a table in the back of the room and, other times, I sit at the student tables but float around the room.

I had a few technical difficulties on my "maiden voyage." One time the camera got stuck facing away from me because I must have walked too fast for the tracker to connect with the Swivl camera. Another time, while working with a small group of students at a table across the room, a boy's head at another table was in the way of some of my group. When the students sit on the floor, the camera skimmed the tops of their head because I was wearing the teacher remote and it was focusing on me and I could not see the students well. I then figured out I could hang the remote from my pocket to get the camera to focus on the students sitting on the floor, but I should have brought the other microphones to the floor rather than leaving them on the tables. I was doing these adjustments without trying to take away from my teaching. I think I have some of the kinks worked out and will be ready to try another video session. I definitely need to zoom out and find the best location to set the camera to see all the students and most of the classroom.

I did reflect on my videos and found it interesting to watch myself teach. I taught a math lesson about making patterns, recognizing patterns with cubes and applying knowledge of skip counting to draw out a pattern further. I noticed that a few kids were actually focused on the Swivl camera rather than the lesson. The students were all curious about what the camera was doing and who would be in view. Some students would look back at the camera and then finally moved out of the way to not be in the camera shot. Overall, my lesson was effective and engaged some of the students but not all of the students. I try to get all students engaged in the math discourse but that does not always happen. If I did the lesson over, I might break the group up into 2 smaller groups to access all students in discussion. But, because of time constraints, that is not always possible. The strong students tend to dominate the discussion, which sometimes skips right over the heads and understanding of students that struggle.

I also video-recorded a math lesson where the students used their notebooks to respond to the question I was asking. I then looked around and found some good examples to share with the class to give the students that need more guidance ideas on how they could show and organize their thinking. I noticed the students that really needed to hear what I said did not stop writing and look to see what I was showing them. Using the notebooks requires all the students to be thinkers and document their thinking for me to see, even if they did not get called on to answer a question.

During math lessons, I like to spend time with math discourse to help students with explanations and sharing their thinking. I think I have done a good job fostering positive conversations within our work time. I ask good questions and I repeat what students say during explanations or ask another student to repeat explanations. I ask for multiple ways to show work and celebrate those ways. I give students think time by not calling on the first hand that is raised and try to choose a variety of students to call on. I still tend to have a few stragglers that do not participate in discussions, and those students are most likely the struggling students or distracted students.

I also video-recorded a guided reading lesson with a small group of students. I introduced a new book that was about future homes. The students loved to see examples of possible homes in the future, even a home on the moon. We looked at text features of a non-fiction book and discussed what they thinking. The lesson went well, but I felt I should have wrapped up the lesson sooner to give the students more independent reading time. Then that would allow me to rotate more groups through their guided reading lessons during our reader's workshop time.

One of my biggest challenges at the primary level, grades 1-2, is making sure everyone is engaged in their learning. On a daily basis, I work with students that are learning to work independently, but are not able to sustain focus without adult interventions. That is very typical for the grades I teach, but I always strive to keep everyone's focus on their work. I sometimes get interrupted during guided reading lessons to help a student with an iPad log in issue or someone does not understand their word study sort, even after teaching the sorting lesson. It is an art to continue to balance the needs of all students while still focusing on a guided reading lesson. I have a few students who have to be watched like a hawk to make sure they keep their focus, stay in their seat and get their work done. I have learned to be a flexible teacher and multitask throughout my day.

This is my first video-recording reflection. There is always room for improving my teaching and I am excited to share a video with you. Please let me know if this is enough detail for your needs. I believe the next step is to meet…with you to discuss a goal and then videotape another lesson. I look forward to hearing back from you. Thank you.

And Jim's response…

Dear Michael,

Many, many thanks for your wonderful reflection!

We both have experiences in Syracuse…I was a teacher and an administrator in Liverpool during '78-'87 and my daughter was the '85 Onondaga County New Year's Baby…small world!

You have such a wonderful breadth and depth of experience! Your PE degree is also noteworthy…PE and Music teachers do a terrific job of checking for understanding, modeling, and giving feedback!

I applaud that you did several self-reflections to give you reflections on your instruction throughout a given day...much applause!

Many thanks for your patience and flexibility with the technology....we are in a pioneering effort and I am so appreciative of your patience and understanding as these wrinkles surface and then get ironed out.

Regarding your very thoughtful reflections on your videos:

--Really liked that you found exemplars of excellence from student work and shared them...It is vital that students know what success looks like

--You give students 'think time'/reflection time but you notice that some students do not participate in the activity as much as you would like from time to time

--You are very attentive to the 'balancing act' required when giving a guided reading lesson

Our next step is to focus in on a key area for your next video where you think I can best help you as your coach. Let me think out loud for a minute and give my 'two cents'.....actively engaging all students in think time/reflection time might be an area where we can partner up. Making all students' thinking visible throughout the lesson is a key area that you have reflected on. Here's a link to Doug Lemov's technique that he calls "Show Me" (Lemov, 2010): http://teachlikeachampion.com/blog/dani-quinn-uses-show-check-understanding/

The video shows a teacher engaging students with whiteboards/slates....admittedly, they are older kids, but I invite you to check out the video and narrative to consider how all your students might use whiteboards to demonstrate their thinking in an overt way.

This is just one thought....voice and choice are key to our work.....Let me know what area you might want to focus in on when you video a 10-15 lesson segment and send me some good times/dates for me to give you a call or a Skype to wrap our arms around this before your video.

Michael, many, many thanks for your wonderful reflections! It is my good fortune to work and learn with you!

Cheers!

Jim

An excerpt from another self-reflection:

As I was watching the video I noticed there are a few things I would like to change before I record my next lesson. I tend to stand on the left side of my SmartBoard while I am teaching so I should move the Swivl to the opposite side of the room because there are many shots where I am blocking the view of the SmartBoard. Also, you can hear the microphone clicking on my ID badge in the video so I should remove it. Considering one of my major goals for the school year is to improve discourse in my instruction, I need to find a better way to utilize the microphones when the kids "turn and talk" and share out their answers.

I was surprised how often I repeated some of the same phrases in such a short period. I know "turn and talk" is a great strategy to increase discourse, but I think I need to find different ways to word it because it seemed repetitive to me - so it must feel that way to the kids, too. Next lesson I would like to try to use different phrases for the same concept - talk to your partner, chat with your table, share what you think, etc.

I was trying to walk around to get a full view of the class in the video but there were a few times when it looked like I was walking around with very little purpose. I tend to skim the room and check their work/ conversations, but I do not usually have a specific goal when I walk around. I just hope to see or hear something that is worth sharing or notice something that might need to be corrected/addressed in the conversation. When I walk around to listen to the kids, I want to get more involved and encourage the conversations. I tend to only chime in if they need to make a correction, but I would like to spend more time listening to students' explanations even when they have the right answer.

Like I mentioned earlier, if I could do a retake I would like to change some of the phrases I use when encouraging students to have a conversation about math. I would also like to change the way I modeled that example on the board. It was hard to hear the students sharing their answers, but it seemed like I spent a lot of time shading in that array when the students were already done. I know I do not want to give the answer away when they are working, but maybe I could have the model ready to show on the board instead of spending time during the lesson to fill it out.

I cannot believe how much this 10-minute video has made me think!

And Jim's response:

Thank you so much for your very informative and wonderful note!

Was great to read that you engage kids with flexible groups....all too often I've seen kids suffer the "Hotel California" syndrome when placed in a group...'you can check in, but you can never check out !" So refreshing to see a much more positive mindset!

Your reflections are compelling, candid, and most informative!

I like your mentioning the Tech Reflection piece...we are pioneering these efforts so this feedback is so helpful! I'm sure Dr. Mike and his team are most appreciative! Thanks!

I am thrilled that your "Self-Reflections" gave you a lot to reflect on...much applause!

As your coach, let me think out loud a bit regarding...Turn and Talk and Monitoring students when they are at work.

First...Turn and Talk...

This is a fine strategy to engage everyone in discussing the content with a partner. Here is a link to this topic:

http://www.theteachertoolkit.com/index.php/tool/turn-and-ta

A point of interest in this link is a way to vary this idea via: "Eyeball Partners," Shoulder Partners, and Clock Partners...

This helps take away the overuse of the term "Turn and Talk" when we engage students - and interweaving a variety of these strategies might help students increase their focus.

A close partner of Turn and Talk is "Think/Pair/Share"---I like this technique because we engage students with "Thinking" before turning and talking or pairing and sharing. We can make this "Thinking" covert or overt.....With covert you just ask students to think about the answer...give some wait time and then they share....but with overt you have them make their thinking visible...maybe they have to jot down their thoughts...maybe they have to draw a picture of their thoughts, etc...as they do this you can walk around to monitor who is understanding, who isn't, see where the learning gaps are, etc...it holds all students accountable and in a way acts as a "Ticket to Talk"...then students share with a partner....

Now to monitor students when they are working...

I'm not sure if you guys have Teach Like a Champion 2.0....or The Field Guide for Teach Like a Champion 2.0 (Lemov, 2015)...but Doug Lemov unpacks a powerful idea with the technique called Tracking, Not Watching

Here is a link to a summary of this idea:

http://teachlikeachampion.com/blog/coaching-and-practice/tracking-not-watching-field-guide-2-0-excerpt/

If you get a chance, check into some of these resources as you reflect on how I can best help you as your coach with your next taping of 10-15 minutes of instruction.

Because your reflections were so thoughtful and so informative, it really helped me as your coach....much applause!

After digesting all this good stuff, send me an e-mail with some good possible times/dates where we can set up a phone or Skype conversation to finalize the focus of the lesson you will video record.

It is my very good fortune to be your coach and colleague!

Many thanks!

And one more:

I joined this Video Coaching program as I felt it would be a great way to reflect on the practices I am currently using. This is my tenth year of teaching and I am also hosting my first student teacher. It has been great to not only reflect on what strategies and tools I use most often but also be able to share what has worked with my student teacher. I think video coaching will be a great way for me to reflect on myself as I ask this soon-to-be teacher to do the same thing! Looking forward to this experience and working with you.

Reflection:

My self-reflection was a math lesson on fractions. As I watched the short clip I noticed a few things. The focus was multiplying fractions, but more specifically we are focusing on the question: "What do you already know about the answer before solving?" I thought I did a nice job anchoring the students into this target and idea. I also continued to come back to this question throughout the lesson which helped the students to almost predict it was coming and be ready to respond to each example. We use specific math-talk strategies such as "turn and talk" and "stop and jot" which the kids are familiar with. Utilizing turn and talk is a nice way to engage the students, keep them accountable and also help them work to communicate their ideas clearly and think flexibly when their partner suggests something else. If I were to do a "retake," I would keep the same focus question and use of "turn and talk." In terms of a small change, I would perhaps spend more time on one of the examples that really drove home the target for the lesson and maybe have kids do a personal exit slip or reflection so I had some specific evidence for each student. The turn and talk was great to hear from each group/table but wouldn't necessarily give me specific information on understanding by each student.

Looking forward to corresponding with you and recording more videos for reflection.

Jim's response:

Thank you for your wonderful note!

Your work sounds very exciting and the opportunity to team each day with another colleague gives you many opportunities to share and reflect together!

You are 'on the money' when you indicate that a key feature of our work is using self-reflection from the video and then partnering with a coach or colleague to unpack those reflections, try to figure out what the mean, and then determine how should we proceed next with our students.

Turn and talk definitely holds students accountable and gives students important practice with communication skills. As students are turning and talking and we walk around the room listening to student discussions and giving feedback where needed, it also provides us invaluable formative assessment data....lets us know who is understanding the concept, who isn't, where are the confusions, etc.

You are very astute in using this technique to take the information you gained where students demonstrated key ideas.

As your coach, I want to affirm the direction you are headed and have you think about the focus on what you do after the "Turn and Talk"....how you utilize what you learned about degrees of student understanding, etc., and use that to either make some adjustments in your instruction or delve deeper into a topic or two.

Here are a couple of thoughts/videos from Doug Lemov on the technique of "Turn and Talk" (Lemov, 2010)....they may or may not be helpful but they do provide some interesting commentary on this technique...will look forward to hearing your thoughts!

http://teachlikeachampion.com/blog/video-review-getting-the-most-out-of-the-turn-and-talk/

http://teachlikeachampion.com/blog/like-turn-talk-much-next-guy/

If you get a chance, take a look at them and then give me some good times/dates where we can have a phone conversation (am still working on getting some hiccups out of Skype) to further explore your ideas for taping a lesson segment ...and also your thoughts about Lemov's videos/commentary.

Big Idea #4 - Choose carefully the best way to respond to the first "real" video-recorded lesson.

You check your email and...yes! A teacher has sent their first video to you via Swivl.

There are two versions of how the coach can respond.

<u>Version 1</u>

Previously, you will have conveyed to the teacher that, when you meet to review the video recorded lesson, you will be asking:

- On a scale of 1-10, how effective was the lesson and why? Be ready to show evidence from the video of why you gave the rating you did.

- What do you want to do to make the next video closer to a 10, and how can your coach best help you to get there?

To prepare for this conference, you will need to review the reflections between you and the teacher to focus in on and be mindful of the goal or goals chosen for concentration and if there is anything the teacher indicated they would like to pay special attention to.

Next, we strongly suggest "The Power of 3" — three viewings of the video recorded lesson.

1. Viewing 1 - Keeping in mind all of the above considerations, watch the lesson from beginning to end. Like reading a book or watching a movie, initially, do not take any notes. Just watch it. Let the story unfold. Take in the key elements from the lesson, watching for that area the teacher wants to work on and what she has asked you to notice.

2. Viewing 2 - During this second viewing, Jim jots down notes at specific time stamp moments in the lesson where he wants to consider the impact of the teaching on learning, especially those moments that define a goal on which the teacher is working and/or has asked for specific feedback. Discovering more about the story of this lesson, the story of the students,

and the story of the relationship between the teacher and their students also are so important at this juncture. This also is where Jim begins to find possible articles, videos, research, etc., that he might link into his commentary to offer strategic support that will make sense to the teacher.

3. Viewing 3 - Now view the video for a final time. Again, jot down notes about moments during the lesson related to the teacher's instructional goal and/or where the teacher has asked you to pay special attention. As you do this final review, you can interject your own thoughts as to where you think this lesson falls on a 1-10 scale and why — not, necessarily, to reveal to the teacher but to compare your assessment with the teacher's self-assessment when you meet. During this final viewing, take a deep dive into your instructional toolbox and be prepared to help the teacher explore key ideas that come up in the reflective process. This is helpful when moving the discussion to the all-important question, "What do you want to do with the next lesson video to get it closer to a 10 — and how can I, as your coach, best help you?"

Version 2

You previously have conveyed to the teacher that you will be reviewing the video several times and offering time-stamped commentary on the lesson where you will pose more questions than offer suggestions. You will send that commentary to the teacher for review and reflection, then schedule a time to reflect together — the teacher's take on the lesson as well as thoughts about the coach's commentary.

We use Swivl to have the video sent and where Jim can add commentary. It is important to note here that the teacher must have total control over how the video is sent and to whom. A teacher participant can use it only for self-reflection, can send it to the coach, or — possibly — can send it other colleagues with Swivl accounts. At this point in time, we are using this version primarily for teacher self-reflection and sending video to the coach, but we are hopeful that we can expand this idea into collegial teams of teachers engaged in video-recorded lessons for the purpose of improving instruction. This concept is outlined in Jim Knight's book, *Focus on Teaching: Using Video for High-Impact Instruction* (Knight, 2014).

With the use of Swivl, we again recommend that you give the video three viewings as outlined in Version 1. The third viewing, however, includes the coach's time-stamped commentary with a special focus on the area on which the teacher is working and where the teacher has asked for your help. A positive with Swivl is the ability to include links to articles, videos, etc., with your commentary. In our experience, teachers truly appreciate the concrete reference to an effective strategy they may be able to add to their instructional toolboxes.

When Jim writes his first commentary with a participant, he attempts to present 5 "glows" to every "grow," terminology we borrowed from a platform we originally used called "Smarter

Cookie" (no longer in business, unfortunately). We were concerned teachers might find this labeling negative, but — across the board — they have found commentary points identified in this way very helpful.

Before Jim sends out the commentary to the teacher, he reads it over several times, putting himself in the shoes of the teacher who will be reading it: "Does it honor her work? Do I respond to the goals on which the teacher is focusing? Am I responding to the areas for which they have asked assistance? Is the commentary positive and professional in its tone? When offering a 'grow,' how do my words land?" Go back to your initial face-to-face meeting with the teacher to gauge what she is "ready to hear" and what may need to wait until you are certain she will accept the feedback in the spirit in which it is being given.

Big Idea #5 - Say less, ask more.

You have sent the commentary to the teacher. Now you set up a time to review the video together.

Before you meet with the teacher, repeat this mantra: "Ask one question at a time."

This is the new habit Jim has developed. After asking a question, instead of adding a clarifying or extending or related question, he stops talking.

One question. Then he waits for the answer.

When you ask, "On a scale of 1-10, how would you rate this lesson?" wait for the answer then wait again after the teacher gives you a number. You have told them in advance that you will ask this question and that you will want to know why they have rated themselves the way they did. When the teacher starts to talk about the why, stay quiet; let the teacher tell their story. If the response is somewhat superficial, say, "Tell me more" or "Say some more about this" to elicit a bit more.

We should point out here (remembering that our coaching is completely confidential and totally non-evaluative), in the hundreds of video conferences in which we have participated, we have never had a teacher give themselves a 9 or a 10 on a video-recorded lesson. In fact, most of the time teachers are very critical of themselves and give a rating in the 5-7 range.

After the teacher offers a number rating for the lesson and provides a rationale for the choice, ask them to take you into the video to show you evidence of effective instruction and places in the lesson where there may have been "choppy water" where instruction did not produce the desired impact on learning on which she was planning. The power here is that the teacher is reflecting on her own instruction as you both relive the story of the lesson.

Following this discussion comes the moment that defines quality professional development. Thanking the teacher for their thoughtfulness and reflection, you ask, "What do you want to work on for the next video recorded lesson that will move your instruction closer to a 10 — and how, as your coach, can I best help you get there?"

A couple of cautions: A mistake Jim made early on with his coaching was viewing the video with the teacher and finding he was doing most of the talking in reviewing his commentary. Teachers would add comments in a limited fashion, thank Jim for the experience, and they were done. In Jim's own self-reflection, he realized he inadvertently set a tone of a more traditional post-observation conference where the unspoken rule was, "Get 'em in, get 'em to smile, get 'em to sign, get 'em out." His very early video conferences were too similar to this outdated, ineffective model. Nothing in this interaction encourages ongoing conversation or the motivation to perform at a higher level.

The adjustment of having the teacher review the video before meeting with the coach and knowing the broad-based questions Jim was going to ask has resulted in his listening to the teacher during the vast majority of their time together. The conference becomes a kind of travelogue of the video where the teacher leads the tour, showing evidence at very specific points in the lesson where their teaching positively impacted student learning (or where it didn't). Because Jim is the coach and not the evaluator, he does not need — or want — to make summative judgments. And because the teacher is in control, she is doing most of the "cognitive heavy lifting" during the conference.

The procedures described above — more than anything — use the observation process as a way to refocus teachers on teaching and open the door for an ongoing discussion about individual teacher's improvement of instruction. The combination of a skilled coach and the judicious use of video-recorded lessons is a sure-fire recipe. Jim's varied and extensive experience as a video instructional coach is the solid evidence upon which we are able to say, without reservation, "This works."

GETTING READY TO BEGIN VIDEO COACHING

So, hopefully, we have you convinced that you want to move forward with implementing a video coaching program in your school. We are excited for you and know that this will be transformational for all involved. Keeping in line with the last chapter, here are our Big Ideas for implementation.

Big Idea #1 – You can start without Swivl.

We have discussed the use of Swivl and it is an outstanding technology that has worked for us. If your school has the financial means to purchase a Swivl robot and licensing for your teachers and coaches, that is great; if not, don't let that prevent you from starting your implementation. Our first go at video coaching utilized an inexpensive video camera that recorded on a DVD. If you are only dabbling in this process you may want to start here. There are many inexpensive technologies available that may meet your need. Teachers can view their teaching and keep notes on a pad or in a Word document. We did find it helpful to note the time of a particular segment of video so we could fast forward or rewind during reflection and conferencing. You can also post your teaching to YouTube by creating a private channel that will only allow you and those you invite to observe your teaching.

Big Idea #2 – Work out your technology kinks ahead of time.

No matter what recording technology you use, make sure that it works the way you would like it to. Set up a meeting with prospective participants to get used to the technology. Allow them to play with it, practicing recording, deleting, and uploading. They should test the audio and so on. In our early days, teachers would become frustrated if they did not hit the record button or accidentally erased the lesson. We also found it beneficial to create quick guides that help with the technology. If at all possible, we found the best results by removing the teacher from the technology set up. What we mean by this is if you have a technology staff member who can become skilled at setting up the camera, tearing it down, and uploading the video, you will find that the teachers are extremely happy with the process. You want the teachers focusing on teaching the lesson, not setting up the technology. So as we mentioned, make sure someone in your technology department becomes experienced with the process.

Big Idea #3 – Discuss your vision with the teachers' association.

It is extremely important to communicate your vision with the leadership of the teachers' association. We have found this group to be some of the biggest advocates for the video coaching program, but it is important for them to understand it; as we mentioned earlier, trust is a critical element to your success. Sitting down with union leadership and demonstrating how this will help a teacher be successful, then providing them an opportunity to ask any questions they may have, will be very beneficial to your process. We are not saying ask permission, but the union's endorsement will help your initiative spread like wildfire. Remember the power of the relationships between teachers. If one teacher has a positive experience, s/he will pass it on, just like anything in life. We found that our programs grow best when teachers share their experiences in the faculty room and at the water cooler. We have harnessed this concept and recently had teachers who have participated in a pilot create an informational video about their experience and present it to their fellow faculty members.

Big Idea #4 – Start with a small group of teachers.

We all want to change the world overnight, but we also know that change takes time. We encourage you to consider this long and hard. We also recommend that you consider choosing teachers who are more open-minded to change and risk-taking. There is a method to our madness. Depending on the size of your district and your technology capacity, this allows you to create cheerleaders for the program and work out any kinks in the process. Once you have tested everything and can answer questions from all stakeholders, you will be ready for full implementation.

Big Idea #5 – Start with an external video coach.

As you have already read, the person you choose to be the video coach needs to be a pretty special person. With that being said, we recommend that you utilize a trusted retired administrator or teacher to become your video coach. Once your program is established, you might look to build capacity by training in-house teachers to become video coaches, but to be respectful to the culture and embrace the strategy of making this change, we almost guarantee utilizing an internal administrator or teacher or coach will fail. We, unfortunately, have experience working with a school and this was exactly the outcome.

Big Idea #6 – Provide appropriate training and resources for your video coach.

In the back of this book, you will find a list of resources we have compiled that will support your coaches' development. We are also available to answer any questions or brainstorm solutions for you on your journey. We recommend focusing on available training for instructional coaches. Jim Knight is one of our favorites. Book studies, professional conversations, and attending instructional coaching conferences will pay dividends. It is important to invest in your initiative on the front end. Assess your coaches' skill set. Would you feel comfortable working with the coach if you were a teacher? You can always slow down and make sure you are prepared to move forward which is preferable to regret it after you have started and you have lost buy-in.

MOVING FORWARD

This chapter provides an overview of key findings from our experience with video coaching. Take this into consideration as you join our journey in moving video coaching to the next level in an effort to give teachers -- and, ultimately, students -- what they truly deserve.

The video coaching approach is a worthwhile program that teachers found added value to their instructional skill set. This was evident, as the number of participants has grown within schools and expanded to multiple districts. We found that all teachers perceived the program to support the improvement of their teaching skills because it provided them a unique opportunity to reflect on their practice with the assistance and mentoring of a video coach.

The relationship that teachers develop with the video coach appears to be most important to the program's success. Every teacher we spoke to discussed at length and in detail how special the relationship was with the coach. Although the act of reflection using video-recording was an eye-opening experience and valuable in itself, ultimately the quality and skill set of the video coach and the approach that he took to make the teachers comfortable and willing to be risk-takers in this process were directly related to the success of their experience. We heard that the coach's instructional knowledge and experience with teaching and learning, combined with his personality and personal approach, made their coaching sessions very positive.

In addition to the value that the teachers experienced from being able to see themselves teach on video and the assistance the coach provided in the reflection process through building a quality relationship, several characteristics stood out as relevant to the program. These included that the program was non-evaluative, confidential, optional, ongoing in fashion, and reflective. Teachers recognized a significant level of trust that was established between the coach and themselves during the coaching cycle. Teachers confirmed that these traits were believed to be essential to the program's success, and that is why they have been named the special ingredients in the secret sauce. We believe they are the glue of the program.

The implementation and growth of the program have been unique in nature. The video coaching approach initially began with the administration reaching out to a few teachers to pilot early in the concept. After two years, the number of participants grew substantially. Teachers indicated that there could be multiple reasons for the growth of the program, including the variables of reflection, the relationship with the coach, or the special ingredients, but all teachers found it necessary to explicitly share the organic or grassroots growth of the program through teachers telling teachers about the program and encouraging them to participate.

When we implemented the video coaching approach it was a third-party individual who had a strong background in teaching and learning and was not familiar with the teachers and administration in the school. We used this strategy because we wanted to ensure that the program was non-evaluative and confidential. This is important during implementation because it helps remove many concerns about the program.

The primary strength of the video coaching approach is the coaching that the teachers receive during the reflection process from the video coach and the relationship that the two parties develop. One of the most frequently recognized traits of the coach that was communicated by teachers was the coach's ability to make teachers feel comfortable with the process. They confirmed that the coach was humble, kind, and took the time to establish a relationship of trust with each instructor, which supported the teacher's vulnerability required to have the most effective coaching process. The coach served as an expert who had the skills, knowledge, and experience to help teachers come to their own conclusions about their teaching.

Another strength of the video coaching program was the opportunity for the teachers to see themselves teach on video. The data indicated that all participants perceived being able to see what they looked like when teaching and the viewpoint of what their students experienced when being instructed as an essential element to improve their instruction. The ability to pause, rewind, replay, and mark sections of the video was indicated to be beneficial in the reflection process. Teachers shared that when reviewing the video with the coach they embraced the function of being able to pull up specific segments of video-recorded instruction to discuss. They found a benefit in including an iPad or a SmartBoard in the post-recording meeting, with which they viewed the video-recording together.

The strength of the relationship of the video coach with the participants and the skill set of the coach have implications. This relationship was noted as an integral part of the video coaching program. For a video coaching program to be successful, a district considering implementation should be thoughtful in the recruitment and retention of a video coach. Districts should take the appropriate time and resources to have the coach trained in the skills necessary to be a good video coach.

The reflective process that takes place when observing oneself teach on video was perceived as very positive. Yet there is the potential for teachers to become desensitized to seeing themselves on video. It is also possible that teachers will elect to use video outside of their relationship with the video coach to improve their practice by themselves or with a colleague. Although there is a considerable amount of literature on the benefits of reflection, teachers will benefit more from a structured guide to the reflection process.

The video coaching approach reestablishes an environment of safe risk-taking and a mindset of improving teaching practices. If your goal of implementing a video coaching program is the same, we recommend continued support for the essential elements of success.

First, when initially implementing the video coaching program, you should not stray from our original design, which included a process that is non-evaluative, confidential, embedded, ongoing, and optional. A third-party video coach is optimal, but using internal coaches may be a realistic solution to build capacity if implemented in a thoughtful manner. Concrete and intensive training should be provided for current and future coaches. This training is necessary and must be ongoing and embedded into the work of the coach. New coaches should work with an experienced video coach. This training must include the goal of the participants understanding the application of instructional strategies. The coaches-in-training will need to provide evidence of both understandings and be able to explain these strategies, as well as possess the ability to model and apply them successfully for teachers to see. Another strand of this training should include learning activities focused on building relationships and understanding how the actions of the coach are integral to the success of the video coaching program. Instructional strategies within the video coaches' training should include role-playing, the fishbowl approach we discussed earlier, and self-reflection with video.

Second, all new hires to your school should be allowed and encouraged to participate in the video coaching approach. Just before hiring a new teacher or during the interview process, it is important to gauge the candidate's openness to the approach. Before we gave the final offer to a finalist, we would confirm participation in video coaching so there were no surprises. A video coaching overview should be created and provided by teachers who are currently involved in the approach, as well as the district's video coaches, to be presented at new teacher orientation. A similar model should be designed and presented at faculty meetings in each building to encourage current faculty to participate and develop themselves with a full understanding of the program and its intended purposes. Teachers are more willing to participate if their colleagues are sharing how beneficial the approach is compared to the message being given by a supervisor.

Third, a successful coaching approach requires appropriate resources. Although funding is important, clear knowledge of the video coaching process and the amount of time necessary to meet with participants to review and comment on the video-recordings is critical. Look to maximize the time a coach works with teachers. This may involve unconventional strategies such as adjusting a teacher's day or building a schedule conducive to pre-recording and post-recording meeting times. Technologies such as Skype and Zoom could be used to hold coaching sessions outside of the school day and from different physical locations. This could lead to a more efficient program as it may provide teachers and coaches time outside of the instructional day. If this approach is preferential, it would impact the program by providing teachers more time to reflect and eliminate the stress of fitting coaching sessions into the school day. Establishing a culture throughout the district that recognizes the importance of video coaching will be integral to advancing the program.

Finally, there are numerous challenges with implementing a video coaching approach, but if the financial means are available, the program could be improved if you provide multiple video coaches, each who is a specialist in one of the content areas. This will provide the opportunity for a teacher to reflect on both the content and the strategies used to deliver it with the assistance of a video coach. This recommendation should be noted as ambitious and should be considered over the long term.

Ongoing evaluation of your video coaching approach is necessary and will support the continued improvement of the program. It will be beneficial to collect both qualitative and quantitative data from your teachers who have participated. Once you are seeing success with your initiative, keep in mind the importance of analyzing the video coach-to-teacher ratio to determine if the current model is meeting the needs of your school. This may help to determine if the resources and support in place for the current program are meeting the demand of the work in an effective, efficient, and sustainable manner. This investigation could identify measures for your school to consider when looking to expand a video coaching program and provide insights into the design and budgeting process. It will be necessary to identify and calculate the ratio of both the third party and internal video coaching scenario.

In conclusion, our work has confirmed that teachers who have participated in the video coaching program find it to be beneficial professional development and that it added value to their teaching. The conversations we have had with teachers during our work support the idea that video-recording and reflection on a teacher's instruction are enhanced when working with a video coach and that the video coach's skills are essential to the success of the approach.

We hope you are convinced of the power of video coaching and decide to transform your school for your teachers and students. Thank you for reading our book. If we can be of any assistance, please feel free to contact us at Jtabcman@aol.com or Kosiorekcasey@gmail.com.

ABOUT THE AUTHORS

James Thompson, NAESP Nationally Distinguished Principal and
New York State Elementary Principal of the Year. Jim is a retired
Elementary Principal with 30 plus years of administrative experience.
Jim currently serves as the Executive Director of Video Coaching
for the Genesee Valley Educational Partnership. He served as an
Elementary Principal, Assistant Principal, Social Studies teacher, and
he has taught at the Elementary, Middle School, High School levels,
and 15 years teaching undergraduate and graduate level students. He
has also served as National Consultant for HOPE Foundation
working with districts in Illinois, Michigan, Virginia, Alabama, Kansas
and New York.

Jim has had his work published in the Journal of School
Administrators' Association of New York on topics
including supervision of instruction and the importance of mentoring
for school administrators. He has also been published by the
Association of California School Administrators on the topic of
instructional leadership.

Casey Kosiorek Ed.D, Superintendent of Schools, joined the Hilton
School District on Jan. 1, 2016. Prior to that, he served as
Superintendent of the Byron-Bergen Central School District, a
position he held since 2012. Dr. Kosiorek earned his Bachelor of

Science degree in physical education and Master of Science degree in education from Canisius College. He then earned his Certificate of Advanced Study in Educational Leadership from The College at Brockport and his doctorate in educational leadership at the University of Rochester.

Dr. Kosiorek taught physical education and health at Royalton-Hartland Central School District. During that time, he also coached varsity football, varsity swimming, and modified track. He has worked at Le Roy Central School District's Wolcott Street Elementary School as assistant principal and then principal.

In 2017, Workplace Dynamics, in conjunction with D&C Digital, presented Dr. Kosiorek with the Leadership Award for the Rochester Top Workplace - Large Employers. He has also been named Administrator of the Year by the School Administrators Association of New York State, was recognized for his leadership by the Genesee Valley Association for Supervision and Curriculum Development, and received the Tyll van Geel Educational Leadership Award from the University of Rochester.

Dr. Kosiorek is a member of the National Center for Education Research and Technology and is a member of the New York State Council of School Superintendents.

REFERENCES

Baecher, L., & Kung, S. (2011). Jumpstarting novice teachers' ability to analyze classroom video: Affordances of an online workshop. *Journal of Digital Learning in Teacher Education, 28*(1), 16-26. doi:10.1080/21532974.2011.10784676

Best Foot Forward Project. (2013). Retrieved March 30, 2017, from https://cepr.harvard.edu/best-foot-forward-project

Borman, J., & Feger, S. (2006). *Instructional coaching: Key themes from the literature.* Providence, RI: Brown University, Education Alliance. Retrieved June 6, 2016, from https://www.brown.edu/academics/education-alliance/sites/brown.edu.academics.education-alliance/files/publications/TL_Coaching_Lit_Review.pdf

Covey, S. R. (1989). *The 7 habits of highly effective people.* New York, NY: Simon & Schuster.

Feger, S., Woleck, K., & Hickman, P. (2004). How to develop a coaching eye. *Journal of Staff Development, 25*(2), 14-18.

Felder, R. & Brent, R. (1996). If you've got it, flaunt it: Uses and abuses of teaching portfolios. *Chemical Engineering Education, 30*(3), 188-189.

Gallucci, C., Van Lare, M., Yoon, I. H., & Boatright, B. (2010). Instructional coaching: Building theory about the role and organizational support for professional learning. *American Educational Research Journal, 47*(4), 919-963. doi:10.3102/0002831210371497

Hubbs, D. L., & Brand, C. F. (2005). The paper mirror: Understanding reflective journaling. *Journal of Experiential Education, 28*(1), 60-71.

Joyce, B., & Showers, B. (1982). The coaching of teaching. *Educational Leadership, 40*(1), 4-10.

Joyce, B., & Showers, B. (1996). The evolution of coaching. *Educational Leadership, 53*(6), 12-16.

King, D., Neuman, M., Pelchat J., Potochink, T., Rao, S., & Thompson, J. (2004). *Instructional coaching: Professional development strategies that improve instruction.* Providence, RI: Annenberg Institute for School Reform, Brown University. Retrieved June 11, 2016, from http://annenberginstitute.org/sites/default/files/product/27 0/files/InstructionalCoaching.pdf

King, S. E. (2008). Inspiring critical reflection in preservice teachers. *Physical Educator, 65*(1), 21-29.

Knight, J. (2007). *Instructional coaching: A partnership approach to improving instruction.* Thousand Oaks, CA: Corwin.

Knight, J. (2014) *Focus on teaching: Using video for high-impact instruction.* Thousand Oaks, CA: Corwin.

Lemov, D. (2010). *Teach like a champion: 49 techniques that put students on the path to college.* San Francisco: Jossey-Bass.

Lemov, D. (2015). *Teach like a champion 2.0: 62 techniques that put students on the path to college.* San Francisco: Jossey-Bass.

Romano, M., & Schwartz, J. (2005). Exploring technology as a tool for eliciting and encouraging beginning teacher reflection. *Contemporary Issues in Technology and Teacher, 5*(2), 149-168.

Shewell, J. R. (2013). *Exploring instructional coaches' attitudes and use of the DataCapture mobile application to collect video-based evidence in teacher evaluation* (Doctoral dissertation). Retrieved June 2, 2016, from https://repository.asu.edu/attachments/114432/content/Sh ewell_asu_0010E_13173.pdf

Star, J. R., & Strickland, S. K. (2008). Learning to observe: Using video to improve preservice mathematics teachers' ability to notice. *Journal of Math Teacher Education, 11*(2), 107-125. doi:10.1007/s10857-007-9063-7

Tripp, T., & Rich, P. (2012). Using video to analyze one's own teaching. *British Journal of Educational Technology, 43*(4), 678-704. doi:10.1111/j.1467-8535.2011.01234.x